The Colour of Steam — Volume 9

The Great Eastern Line

by R. C. RILEY

FRONT COVER: A typical Liverpool Street scene with enthusiasts studying train movements from the one time taxicab entrance, 9th April 1957. 'Sandringham' Class 4-6-0 No. 61662 *Manchester United* was built in 1937. This viewpoint in pre-electrification days gave not only the sight of a busy terminus but the all pervading sound of the beating of Westinghouse brake pumps.

LEFT: Thames Wharf Junction, 31st March 1962, with in the middle distance, the main line curving in on the right from Custom House continuing to Canning Town. The double bracket signal controlled the exit from Thames Wharf Yard on the North Woolwich line. Of McKenzie & Holland design the GER lower quadrant arms had long since been replaced by upper quandrants.

REAR COVER: Immaculately groomed Class B12/3 4-6-0 No. 61572 stands on Norwich shed, 31st May 1960, beside Class J15 0-6-0 No. 65462. By coincidence both engines have been privately preserved and are based on the North Norfolk Railway. The 4-6-0 has yet to be steamed but the 0-6-0 has seen several years service on the line in GER or LNER livery. Not visible is the tender cab fitted to No. 65462 at that time a visible reminder that the J15s did much of their branch line work tender first.

This book is dedicated to the memory of Dr. Ian C. Allen.

Designed by Barnabus Design & Print, Truro, Cornwall.
Typeset by TypeStyle, Truro, Cornwall.
Printed by Century Litho, Penryn, Cornwall.
Bound by Booth Bookbinders, Penryn, Cornwall.

ISBN 0-906899-38-9. First Published 1990.

Published by:

ATLANTIC TRANSPORT PUBLISHERS
Waterside House, Falmouth Road, Penryn,
Cornwall TR10 8BE, England.

Atlantic

INTRODUCTION

The extensive network of lines that served North East London, Essex, Cambridgeshire and East Anglia was developed by a number of companies, the oldest of which was the Eastern Counties Railway, whose first line opened in 1839. Other companies quickly followed to exploit the area, notably the Eastern Union Railway, the Norfolk Railway and the East Anglian Railway. By 1854 the Eastern Counties Railway had gradually taken over the working of these different lines and in 1862 the companies were merged to form the Great Eastern Railway. This later absorbed other companies including the Thetford & Watton, Watton & Swaffham Railways and the Felixstowe Dock & Railway Company. The formation in 1893 of the Midland & Great Northern Joint Railway, bringing together a number of smaller companies, created the only serious rival to the otherwise virtually complete monopoly of East Anglian lines by the GER.

The original London terminus, Shoreditch, was not only inconveniently situated for the City but also unable to cope with increased traffic. The GER obtained an Act in 1865 to build a very costly extension to Liverpool Street, eventually opened in 1874-5. This was just in time to handle the greater suburban traffic demands created by extensions to

Walthamstow (and thence Chingford) as well as a more direct route to Enfield Town, which had been rail served by 1849. The new terminus was later known as the West Side after the further development of the East Side station, opened in 1894. Since the Liverpool Street extension inevitably involved the large scale destruction of workers' dwellings, a condition of the Parliamentary Act was that the GER had to provide cheap workmen's tickets to enable the rehoused workers to reach their work in the metropolis. Initially, special workmen's trains were run, the return fare for the 21œ miles from Enfield Town being two old pence or less than a penny in the present coinage. At a later date Workmen's Fares were available on any train reaching London before 8.00 am and such fares, no longer so cheap, were still available into early BR days. The old Shoreditch terminus, latterly renamed Bishopsgate, became a goods station until it was destroyed by fire in 1964.

The Eastern Counties Railway had its first locomotive works at Squirrels Heath near Romford, but in 1848 it made the wise decision to move to a more extensive site at Stratford where an enormous complex of works, engine sheds, carriage sidings and goods yards gradually developed. The original Romford Factory still survives but the building is no longer railway property.

The GER served such important places as Cambridge, Peterborough, Colchester, Ipswich and Norwich, while it also reached Lincoln and Doncaster by means of the GN & GE Joint Line, with running powers through to York. In addition it served several ports and holiday resorts on the Essex, Suffolk and Norfolk coasts. It had many rural branch lines but with the increased use of road vehicles after World War I some of these lost their traffic after the 1923 Grouping in LNER days, a process that gained impetus in BR days even before publication of the Beeching Report. The GER also had shipping interests and was a pioneer in the use of motor omnibuses.

In early BR days GER lines were designated 'The Great Eastern Line', the title chosen for this book, since all the photographs are taken from that era. Steam traction was eliminated from GE lines in September 1962. Acknowledgements are due to John Watling, Vice President of the GER Society, who kindly provided information on carriages and made helpful suggestions on the captions and also to Roger Farrant for information on signalling. I must also thank the late Dr. Ian C. Allen, Richard Hardy, George Powell and the late Roy Vincent, all of whom at one time or another encouraged my interest in Great Eastern matters.

R. C. Riley.

Ten Class B1 4-6-0s, forerunners of a class designed by Edward Thompson later to be increased to 410 engines, were built during the war at which time many GE lines were subject to hostile air attack. Inevitably maintenance suffered and arrival of eight of these simple engines by 1945 went towards easing the situation. When the class eventually went into quantity production, the first twenty to enter service, Nos. 1040-59, were shared between Norwich and Ipswich depots. Intended as general purpose engines, the B1s became initially the main line passenger engines to a large extent displacing the 'Sandringhams'. No. 61311 heads the 5.36 pm Clacton departure on the East Side of Liverpool Street station, 11th May 1957, while a new 1,500 volt dc EMU set (now No. 307126) stands in the adjacent platform awaiting departure to Southend

Victoria. The full Shenfield-Southend electrified service began on 31st December 1956. Prior to that date, 4-6-0s of Classes B1, B12/3 and B17 provided the line's motive power, in practice mostly Class B12/3s. The East Side of Liverpool Street station was opened in 1894, adding eight platforms to the original ten of the West Side station. Recent building development involves large blocks of offices above the East Side station, while the ornate external view of the West Side train shed can no longer be seen.

After the end of the war in 1945, the impoverished LNER announced that all engines were to be painted green. For economy reasons and because of nationalisation this never proceeded very far. However certain 0-6-0T station pilots were so repainted, among them in 1948 No. E8619 (original BR number), a 1904-built

Class J69 chosen as the East Side pilot at Liverpool Street. In this condition it is depicted at North Woolwich while working the RCTS East London railtour, 14th April 1951. It reverted to unlined black in 1953, but nevertheless continued to be kept immaculate and by 1957 it carried the lined black livery. Its crews received modest bonus payments to keep it clean during its periods of inactivity. It is said that one of its occasional duties was to work Newmarket-Epsom horse boxes through the Thames Tunnel to New Cross Gate; if there was sufficient warning a dirty J69 would be substituted! Nevertheless the pristine appearance of the engine was a morale builder to railwaymen and BR earned fare income from those travelling to see it.
(T. B. Owen)

LIVERPOOL STREET

The West Side of Liverpool Street as it will be remembered, free of overhead wires and the Broadgate development some thirty years in the future. However, when the development is complete the interior of the train shed as a listed building should regain some of its former appearance. In the foreground, Hatfield based Class N7/3 0-6-2T No. 69704 heads an empty stock train, while running in ex-Stratford Works. Darlington-built 'Sandringham' Class B17/6 4-6-0 No. 61618 *Wynyard Park* stands at the head of the 10.40 am parcels train to Ipswich, 4th October 1958. The 'Sandringhams' were introduced to GE lines in 1928 to meet an urgent need for larger engines to work heavier trains. The engine had to come within the confines of the GER loading gauge and, with its tender, be short enough to fit on existing turntables and also meet an axle loading of 17 tons, with which latter requirement it failed to comply. After some design work at Doncaster, responsibility was handed over to the North British Locomotive Company, which in the event built only the first ten engines. By 1935, nearly fifty engines were in service on GE lines named after country seats, later members of the class with football club names being allocated to the GC Section. All were concentrated on the GE Section by 1949.

The West Side of Liverpool Street station, 11th May 1957, with 'Sandringham' Class B17/6 4-6-0 No. 61622 *Alnwick Castle* heading the 3.33 pm departure to Yarmouth South Town, when that resort could boast through services to and from London before the East Suffolk Line was threatened with closure; following intense opposition the south end of the line was reprieved but Yarmouth South Town closed in 1970. Beside the express can be seen Class N7/4 0-6-2T No. 69614, which took up the duty of West Side Pilot at Liverpool Street in 1956 and No. 68619 the East Side Pilot. At right is the stock of the 3.30 pm 'Broadsman' express to Norwich.

In their shaded position under the station roof, it was not possible to do photographic justice to the Liverpool Street pilots so one relatively slack Saturday afternoon, 11th May 1957, I asked Ted Carron, local Running Foreman, if he would be kind enough to arrange for them to be turned to face into the sun. Rather to my surprise he agreed to do so, providing a unique photograph and

giving the youthful observers on the taxicab road an unexpected treat. What a splendid sight these two engines made in contrast to the distant Class B1 on the turntable. The crews earned their one hour's overtime payment to keep these engines in this condition. No. 69614 was West Side Pilot from 1956 until the end of 1960 when electrification of GE suburban lines was completed and there was no longer a need for it. In October 1961, No. 68619 was replaced by an equally well groomed, but destined to be shorter-lived, diesel locomotive. A year earlier Parkeston's Class J69 0-6-0T No. 68633 was withdrawn and was sent into Stratford Works for restoration as GER No. 87. It was initially exhibited at the Museum of British Transport, Clapham and later at the National Railway Museum, York. It is said to be due to be moved to a position inside the restored Liverpool Street train shed on completion of rebuilding works there. The J69s were worthy contenders for preservation as they had once born the brunt of working the well known GE 'Jazz Train' services on the Enfield Town and Chingford lines.

LIVERPOOL STREET

The introduction of the BR 'Britannia' Class 4-6-2s to the Great Eastern in 1951 enabled considerable accelerations to take place on East Anglian lines and a recast timetable was introduced with hourly fast trains between London and Norwich, loaded to nine coaches, and hourly semi-fast trains. No less than 22 were shared between Stratford and Norwich and for a short while, the down 3.30 pm 'Broadsman' from Liverpool Street covered the 115 miles to Norwich in two hours, so briefly attaining the status of the fastest train in the country in place of the WR's 'Bristolian', although the latter region quickly responded by accelerating its train over an easier route! Because of difficulties at Stratford, responsibility for maintenance of

the class was taken over by Norwich shed in 1958 and the entire GE Line allocation was transferred there the following year until the introduction of main line diesels displaced them in 1961. The Norwich Shedmaster responsible for them at that time, Mr. D. W. Harvey, has stated that of the original eight engines placed in his care (Nos. 70006-13), their average annual mileage over ten years was nearly 73,000. One of these, No. 70012 *John of Gaunt* in the then usual immaculate condition, stands at the head of the 3.30 pm 'Broadsman' at Liverpool Street, 2nd May 1958.

One of the 1921-built GE Class N7 0-6-2Ts No. 69604, rebuilt with round topped firebox and then allocated to Wood Street, Walthamstow approaches the terminus on one of the 'Jazz Train' services from

Chingford, 4th October 1958, with two of Gresley's 'Quint-Art' coach sets, ie five coach articulated sets. The first eleven of this class, of which No. 69604 was one, were fitted with Westinghouse brake only. An unusual feature of this photograph is that N7s normally ran chimney first out of the station as they faced the steep climb to Bethnal Green and this engine was the only exception to the rule at the time. When No. 69614 appeared highly polished as West Side Pilot, the Enfield Town men followed suit in grooming their engines, but No. 69604 was the only Wood Street engine so treated.

In September 1959, No. 68619 returned to Stratford to be given the full treatment of GER blue livery, in which form it re-entered traffic on 2nd October 1959, having first been on display at a Colchester Trades Fair from 25th to 28th September. Appropriately, one of its first duties was to attach a former GER Dining Car of 1913 build to a Newmarket race train. In their days on the 'Jazz Trains' these sturdy little 0-6-0Ts earned the nickname of 'Buckjumpers', said to relate to their fast entry to stations, judicious application of the brake at the right moment followed by their quick acceleration away.

Although No. 68619 carried the BR insignia on the side tanks in this condition, it also carried the GER coat of arms beneath the number on the bunker.

STEAM SUBURBAN

Class N7/5 0-6-2T No. 69663 leaves Liverpool Street for Enfield Town, 4th October 1958. This view shows the economy of the Gresley articulated stock, sharing a bogie between two carriages. The building towering above the engine was the old Broad Street station signal box. The former North London Railway terminus at Broad Street was closed in June 1985 and demolished as part of the Broadgate redevelopment project. Trains initially used a temporary platform north of the former station but in June 1986 were diverted into Liverpool Street by means of a new curve at Graham Road, Hackney. The last Stratford-built Class N7 No. 69621, in 1924 and withdrawn in 1962, survives in preservation at Chappel and Wakes Colne on the Stour Valley Line. After 27 years it was triumphantly returned to steam in 1989.

To this day Liverpool Street is the most heavily trafficked terminus in London. By 1919, the overcrowding problem was so serious that drastic action was needed. Under General Manager Sir Henry Thornton, Mr. F. V. Russell, later Superintendent of Operations, took steps to improve matters. By track rearrangements to avoid conflicting movements, signalling alterations and the provision of short engine sidings, the ultimate step in steam operated suburban services was put into effect at a cost of £80,000 compared with an estimated £3 million for electrification. On the coaches the class of travel was denoted by a colour code at door top level, thus earning these services the 'Jazz Trains' title. At the time there were only two 0-6-2Ts in service and the trains were worked largely by Class J69 0-6-0Ts with some assistance from 2-4-2Ts and 0-4-4Ts. In this photograph Class N7/5 0-6-2T No. 69658 has brought in a train from Enfield Town and on departure of its stock, then moved into the engine siding in readiness to take out the next Enfield Town departure, 11th October 1958.

The Thompson Class L1 2-6-4Ts were less successful than the B1 4-6-0s and suffered from axlebox and motion wear that gave rise

to a clanking that enabled them to be identified in the distance without actually seeing them! The L1s had 5ft 2in coupled wheels, 4in larger than the N7s and only 1in larger than the former GCR 2-6-4Ts which were largely employed on freight trains. Those L1s on GE lines were divided between Stratford, Bishops Stortford, Ipswich and Norwich. The Stratford engines were largely used on trains between London and Bishops Stortford or Hertford East. No. 67735 was seen leaving Stratford on a Hertford East via Lea Bridge train on 6th March 1958. With electrification of these lines in November, fourteen were rendered superfluous and withdrawn, but eleven survived at Stratford until steam working ceased in September 1962, latterly being seen on such humble duties as the North Woolwich-Palace Gates service. In pre war days the GE Lines had an allocation of Gresley's lively Class V1 2-6-2Ts with better adhesion qualities.

NORTH WOOLWICH BRANCH

Class N7/5 0-6-2T No. 69640 heads a Palace Gates train out of North Woolwich on 24th June 1961. The listed Grade II station building at North Woolwich, opened by the Eastern Counties Railway in 1847, was built in 1854 replacing a wooden structure provided for the opening. After a period of dereliction the station was transferred to the custodianship of the Passmore Edwards Museum Trust which, with enthusiastic co-operation from the GER Society, restored it to a high standard; following conversion it was re-opened as a railway museum by Her Majesty the Queen Mother in November 1984. Administered by the London Borough of Newham, admission is free and no GER enthusiast should fail to visit it. Note among the cranes and the dockland houses the funnel of a Cunard liner, probably the RMS 'Ivernia' built in 1955.

The Gas Light & Coke Company established the largest gas works in Europe on the marshes north of Gallions Reach which took its name of Beckton from the Company's Governor, S. A. Beck. Although coal to the works was always offloaded from coastal colliers on the Thames, there was a need for a rail connection and the Company provided this in 1871 as far as Custom House on the North Woolwich branch, the GER leasing this from 1874. This unusually terse but meaningful sign was recorded on the Beckton branch, 24th August 1957.

The rugged little J15 Class 0-6-0s designed by T. W. Worsdell were introduced in 1883 and construction continued until 1913, by which time 289 had been built, by far the largest class on the GER. Intended for goods working, notably for coal trains from the Yorkshire coalfields over the GN & GE Joint Line, their low axle loading made them ideal branch line engines and the last 40 built had passenger train brakes and screw couplings. No. 65476 was one of these engines and was recorded shortly before the end of steam with a local freight on the North Woolwich line entering Cohen's Yard, near Abbey Mills Junction, Canning Town on 17th March 1962. *Photograph: K. L. Cook.*

BETHNAL GREEN

'Sandringham' Class B17/6 4-6-0 No. 61656 *Leeds United* climbs Bethnal Green bank with the 12.33 pm Liverpool Street-Yarmouth South Town, 28th February 1959. The 'Sandringham' design came from the urgent need for more modern motive power on GE lines having regard to the fact that at that time axle loading could not exceed 17 tons. When the class was built this proved to be 18 tons, which reduced their route availability. 48 engines were built in this form with short tenders not unlike those on the B12 Class. The last 35 of the class, initially with football club names, had larger tenders and only reached GE lines after use on the GC Section. These three-cylinder engines were renowned rough riders, notably when attaining a high mileage ex works. A March driver, in charge of No. 61657 *Doncaster*

Rovers shortly before withdrawal, told me that he was in charge of it on the Newcastle-Parkeston Quay train and claimed that it was frightening at speeds over 60 mph — he thought when running down a bank the engine was trying to get on to the adjacent track. No. 61657 and the two other remaining survivors of the class were withdrawn in June 1960.

'Britannia' Class 4-6-2 No. 70034 *Thomas Hardy* passes Bethnal Green on time on the up 9.45 am express from Norwich, 28th February 1959. The down suburban train is a Chingford local in charge of Class N7/4 0-6-2T No. 69604, by this time facing correctly chimney first out of Liverpool Street. Behind the carriages can be seen the sawtooth station canopies much beloved of the GER and still to be seen, notably at Ipswich and March. Those at Bethnal Green have only recently been demolished.

As part of his standardisation measures, Thompson rebuilt one of Gresley's Class K4 2-6-0s, long associated with the West Highland Line, to a two cylinder engine, forming the prototype of Class K1. It was left to his successor, Peppercorn, to modify and put into service the 70 engines of the K1 Class in 1949/50. Thirty of these engines were allocated to March enabling the last Gresley Class K2 2-6-0s finally to leave GE lines after a 25 year association. Stratford invariably poached country engines at week-ends, even in the winter, and thus the last of the class, No. 62070, is seen passing Bethnal Green station with a down empty stock train, 28th February 1959. Mostly these engines were to be found on the lighter freight trains between Whitemoor Yard, March and Temple Mills Yard, Stratford, heavier trains being handled by Class 01 or 02 2-8-0s allocated to March.

STRATFORD

Running repairs were carried out in a small two road shed free of the smoke that always seemed to fill the main sheds. It was noticeable that this always dealt with a large proportion of former GER engines. Thus in this picture on 7th May 1961 can be seen Class N7 0-6-2T No. 69697, J68 0-6-0T No. 68649, J15 0-6-0 No. 65460, Class J20 0-6-0 No. 64676 and J19 0-6-0 No. 64657. Also in the shed but not visible were a B1 4-6-0, a J20 0-6-0, a J15 0-6-0, two J69 0-6-0Ts and another N7 0-6-2T. There were two running sheds at Stratford described by Richard Hardy as: "the New Shed, built in the 1870s, and the Jubilee Shed, which was newer, bigger, draughtier, dirtier and on Sunday nights in the summer after lighting up on a large scale, quite intolerable."

Although BR Western Region started the sale of withdrawn steam locomotives to Woodham Brothers, Barry Dock, as early as 1959, it seems likely that most former GER locomotives were broken up at Stratford. What a sight the original *Claud Hamilton* must have made at the 1900 Paris Exhibition in its beautiful Royal Blue livery, its wheel rims and wheel centres burnished and indeed what an impact these 4-4-0s made on the GER motive power scene as the class was multiplied to 121 engines by 1923. From 1933 many of them were rebuilt with boilers having round topped fireboxes and improved front end design, a feature they shared in LNER days with the Class B12 4-6-0s rebuilt to Class B12/3 during Thompson's tenure of office as Assistant Mechanical Engineer, based at Stratford Works. But study No. 62572, built in 1909 and rebuilt to Class D16/3 thirty years later; it was withdrawn from March shed in July 1958 and yet as it stands forlornly awaiting scrap at Stratford, 10th August 1958, it looks remarkably clean — but not quite as clean as it might be as the tender inscriptions testify: "To her last home" and "Farewell old friend". That is surely proof of the popularity of the 'Clauds'. The name, it should be explained, was that of the Chairman of the GER from 1893 until the 1923 grouping. It was not normal GER policy to bestow names on its locomotives.

The completion of electrification of the North East London lines in November 1961 and the conversion of the Shenfield and Southend lines from 1,500 dc to 25kV ac was not accomplished as smoothly as would have been hoped. Indeed BR was forced to

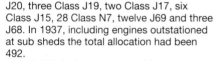

withdraw most of the new EMUs intended for the Enfield, Chingford and Bishops Stortford lines temporarily because of serious electrical faults, attributed in the BR press handout to the contractors. EMUs had to be borrowed from the LT & S Line and from as far afield as Crewe. In this study on 7th May 1961, Driving Trailer No. E75078 (formed in

EMU set No. 302231) is being shunted into the ERS (Engine Repair Shop in GE parlance), there being no other means of access to Stratford Works for EMUs. It is interesting to note that the *Railway Observer* recorded that on completion of this electrification, only 56 steam locomotives were to be retained at Stratford: two Class

J20, three Class J19, two Class J17, six Class J15, 28 Class N7, twelve J69 and three J68. In 1937, including engines outstationed at sub sheds the total allocation had been 492.

A. J. Hill designed a class of five remarkably large and powerful 0-4-0Ts for shunting the various yards in the London area. Built between 1913 and 1921 they eventually formed LNER Class Y4. The last of the class, although given a number in running stock (GER No. 210 and eventually BR No. 68129), in fact was always a departmental engine since it spent its entire life shunting the Old Works at Stratford, outliving the other four engines as it survived until the works closed at the end of 1963. In 1949 it lost its handsome GER chimney for one of the LNER Class N7 pattern and its status was finally recognised in 1952 when it was renumbered 33 in the Departmental series. It was recorded shunting at the Old Works, 6th March 1958. Hill was the last of eight Mechanical Engineers on the GER, these being Sinclair, S. W. Johnson (later on the Midland Railway), William Adams (later on the LSWR), Massey Bromley, T. W. Worsdell (later on the NER), James Holden, responsible for the 'Clauds', S. D. Holden, responsible for the B12s and Hill, who introduced the N7s.

15

STRATFORD

As with the 'Clauds' the Class B12 4-6-0s were rebuilt with larger boilers with round topped fireboxes and improved front end design, 54 of the 80 engines being so treated between 1932 and 1944. Unrebuilt engines were transferred to the Great North of Scotland Section, where their light axle loading permitted them to replace existing 4-4-0s. Their high route availability also proved valuable in wartime when several B12/3s were allocated to SR or GWR sheds to haul air-braked US Army ambulance trains over such unlikely routes as the Somerset & Dorset Line. In early BR years a few were transferred to Grantham and of these No. 61553 had its moment of glory in September 1950 when it replaced an ailing Gresley Pacific on the fourteen coach up 'West Riding Express', which it worked to Kings Cross unassisted, if not on time. It was 'borrowed' by Stratford in the last weeks of Southend Victoria line steam. By 10th August 1958 its days were over and it was on its way to the Scrap Road at Stratford. Unlike some of the foreign engines brought in to work GE lines, the B12/3s were very steady riding.

The James Holden Class E4 2-4-0s,

known as the 'Intermediates', consisted of 100 engines built between 1891 and 1902. Remarkably their maximum axle loading was not on the driving wheels but on the leading wheels, which gave them a marginally smaller route availability than the J15s, although this was honoured probably more in the breach than the observance. Six of the class were sent northwards in 1935 to work the arduous and exposed line from Darlington to Penrith and Tebay over Stainmore summit, where they were found

suitable although the NE enginemen required more cab protection and side window cabs were fitted as seen on No. 62797. They returned to GE lines in 1941-2. No. 62797 put in some of its later years on the milk shunting duties at Halesworth, where I saw it looking commendably clean in October 1956. A few months later it was transferred to Cambridge, where it was said to be in fine fettle even hauling a seven coach train over the Stour Valley line on August Bank Holiday 1957. It was withdrawn in March 1958, and

and Chingford services replacing elderly four wheeled carriages. Some of these had undergone major surgery in the early 1900s when many four wheelers built between 1876 and 1897 were split down the middle and a new section inserted to convert them from five-to-six-a-side seating. The six-a-side stock built new from 1899 onwards was also updated by being paired on new 54ft bogie underframes to form eight coach sets from 1914 onwards. With the 1949 Central Line extensions and the 1949 electrification to Shenfield, many steam suburban sets were displaced. There were 37 Quint Arts on GE lines in LNER days each providing a seating capacity of 872. In peak hours the standing capacity was as important. Here Set 116B stands awaiting scrap, 10th August 1958, the other five coaches concealed in this view would have been Set 116A. It should be mentioned that the LNER-built 'Quint-Arts' for GER lines were Westinghouse brake fitted.

Although it had carried out an extensive programme of converting four wheeled carriages to bogie stock, the GER introduced new bogie suburban stock built in batches between 1911 and 1924 with some variations. While earlier stock was gas lit, later carriages had electric lighting and steam heating. The teak panelling shows to good effect on Nos. 62167 and 62169 in Stratford Carriage Sidings, 18th August 1958. These were two of a batch of four Third Brakes built in 1919 and despite the efforts of local vandals No. 62167 was subsequently converted to Parcels Mail Van No. 6063, although No. 62169 was scrapped. Note the set number on the end of the coach. Despite construction of new suburban carriages and the influx of 'Quint-Arts' to GER lines, the bogie coaches rebuilt from four-wheelers survived on the North Woolwich branch until 1948. Meanwhile the extension of the London Transport Central Line over former GER suburban lines as far as Loughton, including the Fairlop Loop line, was progressively carried out in 1947-8. In September 1949, the Central Line extension reached Epping and although London Transport took over the line thence to Ongar it continued to be worked by steam push and pull trains until 1957. Also in September 1949 the BR electrification from Liverpool Street to Shenfield commenced operation resulting in further withdrawal of steam suburban stock.

by 10th August on the Scrap Road at Stratford it was looking distinctly forlorn.

Also to be seen awaiting scrap at Stratford were displaced carriage sets in the extensive sidings. Gresley had introduced four coach articulated stock to the Great Northern Railway in 1911, referred to as 'Quad-Arts'. When he became Chief Mechanical Engineer of the newly formed LNER in 1923 construction continued of this type of carriage. Five coach sets, known as 'Quint-Arts', were introduced for the Enfield

SIX COUPLED TENDER ENGINES

The redoubtable Class J15 0-6-0s have already been mentioned. One was noted in wartime hauling 100 empty wagons through the admittedly flat terrain of March station without any fuss. In GER days these Worsdell engines were fitted with stovepipe chimneys but the LNER replaced these with cast iron chimneys of NER pattern. In May 1960, Bill Harvey, Norwich Shedmaster, cut the tops off two such chimneys and welded on a beaded rim so giving Nos. 65469 and 65471 a more GER appearance. This was short lived on No. 65471 as it was noted the following month at Colchester en route to Stratford for scrap with a standard chimney, its 'stovepipe' having been transferred to No. 65462, now to be found on the North Norfolk Railway as GER No. 564 No. 65469 was the favoured engine to work special trains and was here noted at the 1846 Listed Grade II Bury St. Edmunds station while running round a Railway Club brake van special, 11th June 1960. The last survivors were mostly from the train braked series, Nos. 65440-79, but 1889-built No. 65361 of Stratford survived until the end of steam on the GER lines in September 1962. No. 65469 had

been withdrawn a month earlier. The GER was the first of the major railway companies taken over at the 1923 grouping of railways to become wholly dieselised or electrified.

James Holden Class J17 0-6-0 No. 65560 repainted at Stratford Works on shed, 11th August 1958. Of the 90 engines built between 1900 and 1911 the earlier engines had round topped fireboxes and 31 of the later engines had Belpaire fireboxes. All were eventually so fitted and superheated. Their boilers were interchangeable with the unrebuilt Class D15 'Claud Hamilton' 4-4-0s as modified with Belpaire fireboxes. Initially used on heavy freight and coal trains until superseded by bigger engines, seventeen were fitted with vacuum ejectors and steam heat to work passenger trains on the GER's rival line in East Anglia, the Midland & Great Northern Joint Railway, working of which was taken over by the LNER in 1936. No. 65567, latterly of Norwich, is preserved at the NRM York in its form as first superheated in 1923 as LNER No. 1217E.

It was a great form of relaxation for me to get away from financial matters in the City and wander round Stratford in an occasional

extended lunch hour. On 6th March 1958 Class J19/2 0-6-0 No. 64671 was recorded in pristine ex works condition. The ten Class J18s, built 1912, and 25 Class J19, built 1916-20, were the first GER goods engines built with superheated boilers. Initially fitted with Belpaire fireboxes, all were rebuilt between 1934 and 1939 with the same type of round topped firebox used on Class D16/3 rebuilds, so forming Class J19/2. Again they started life on the heavy goods trains from Peterborough and March, but in later years the allocation was scattered largely at country sheds.

A. J. Hill, last Locomotive Superintendent of the GER, holding office from 1912 until Grouping, had designed the J18/J19 0-6-0s and built the last word in GER goods engines, the J20 Class, between 1920 and 1922. With most important parts being interchangeable with the unrebuilt B12 Class they were, on a tractive effort basis, the most powerful 0-6-0s in the country until 1942 when Bulleid introduced the austere Q1 Class on the Southern Railway. Although formidable looking engines, there was not sufficient room for them to be rebuilt with Class B12/3 boilers. Nevertheless they were rebuilt with round topped fireboxes but retained their handsome GER appearance. Recently repainted No. 64677 stands over

the ash pits at Stratford, 28th February 1959, with a glimpse of a Gresley Class J39 0-6-0 No. 64784 in the background. Even after introduction of the Gresley Class 02 2-8-0s they could still be seen on heavy freight working between Whitemoor and Temple Mills for many years. Latterly divided between Stratford, Cambridge and March, the last four survivors were withdrawn from the latter shed in September 1962. The '6' on the buffer beam denotes their LNER route availability classification making them the most severely restricted of any GER locomotive.

SIX COUPLED TANK ENGINES

Just as the J20 Class was the ultimate in GER 0-6-0s, so too, the thirty J68 0-6-0Ts were the last of their kind, twenty being built 1912-3 and a further ten by the LNER in 1923. Dimensionally the same as the later series of J69 0-6-0Ts, they could readily be identified by the high roof side window cabs with square spectacle plates. The ten engines built in 1912 were essentially for passenger work, the later engines being intended for shunting, the majority being Stratford based. No. 68649, ex-works, and No. 68665, looking rather more like the run of the mill Stratford shunter, were recorded on 5th June 1958. Both were engines of the shunting series, although of course the first ten built for the 'Jazz Trains' had long been displaced by the N7 0-6-2Ts, the 22 Stratford built examples having been increased in LNER days by a further 112 engines of the class. The J68s became extinct in 1961. Large production of 350hp diesel shunters spelt their doom.

The story of the Class J67/J69 0-6-0Ts in complicated. Indeed a whole book has been written about them. Basically 120 were built for passenger work by James Holden, the original 'Buckjumpers', and 40 were built for shunting duties. They were straightforward at first but then, different boiler pressures, larger side tanks, cabs and bunkers were introduced and interchange of boilers resulted in changes of class. For example ten were downgraded to shunters on construction of the J68s. Inevitably, with the increase in number of 0-6-2Ts, passenger engines became shunters and this is how most now remember them. In early days twenty J69s were transferred to Scotland and indeed they were put to good use throughout the LNER system. Among the Scottish batch was No. 68635, penultimate member of the class built in 1904, which spent fourteen years as station pilot at Perth. It was recorded at Peterborough New England shed on 31st May 1958 and unlike the GE based engines retained a low cab roof and stovepipe chimney. A few survived until the end of steam in 1962. Another 1904 built engine, No. 68633, is preserved as GER No. 87.

EPPING-ONGAR BRANCH

T. W. Worsdell came to the GER from Crewe and in view of the LNWR's partiality for 2-4-2Ts he introduced the type to the GER. Regrettably, the first 40 built in the 1880s were far from successful and their voracious appetite for coal earned them the nickname of 'Gobblers'. Ten were withdrawn by the GER and the rest by the LNER in the 1920s. Meanwhile James Holden built a further 120 2-4-2Ts between 1903 and 1909, these having Stephenson valve gear as used on the J15 0-6-0s with more successful results. Those with 160 lbs boiler pressure were classed F4 and those with 180 lbs were classed F5. Two engines were fitted with side window cabs in 1912, GER Nos. 789/90, later BR Nos. 67218/9. In 1949 seven of these normally Westinghouse brake engines were fitted with vacuum controlled pull and push gear, five being used on the Epping-Ongar branch, the other two on Yarmouth-Beccles and Lowestoft services. Sixteen of these engines were armour plated in 1940 and used on coastal line patrols in armoured gun trains, not only on the East Coast but in North Cornwall, Kent and as far afield as Aberdeen, reverting to normal in 1943. At the same time 36 engines of the class had their chimney height reduced to enable them to work over the London Transport District or Metropolitan lines with GER carriages also set aside in the event of damage to power stations, which in the event did not occur. No. 67218 was one of the side window cab engines of Class F5, recorded at Ongar, 18th May 1957. Six months later the branch was electrified as part of the London Transport Central Line, although the shuttle service from Epping was later restricted to weekday peak hours only. The last steam trains on 16th November 1957 were in charge of Nos. 67200/12/18. The future of the branch is currently being reviewed by London Regional Transport, with all day running on trial for one year.

MALDON BRANCH

The Witham to Maldon branch was opened by the Eastern Counties Railway in 1848 and had a particularly splendid terminus at Maldon East, so named because there was a station at Maldon West on the branch to Woodham Ferrers, affording connection with the Southminster branch and also Southend Victoria, via Wickford, all of these lines opening in 1889. The Woodham Ferrers-Maldon branch lost its passenger service in September 1939 and its freight traffic in 1953, although the spur to Maldon West remained open for goods traffic until 1959. Maldon East retained its passenger service until 1964 and freight train closure followed two years later. Maldon East terminus remains intact and was until recently a restaurant. Class J69 0-6-0T No. 68573 was hauling a Saturday afternoon freight train to Maldon East leaving Witham, 10th May 1958.

On the same afternoon Class J15 0-6-0 No. 65445, recently ex-Stratford Works, heads away from Witham on the 2.45 pm Maldon East train consisting of a composite corridor coach, No. E18477E of Thompson design, now preserved on the North Yorkshire Moors Railway, and 1920 built GER Brake Third No. E62483E. The 8 mph restriction sign refers to trains from the Maldon direction running round the sharp curve into the bay at Witham. Another J15 0-6-0 No. 65470 was in charge of the Witham-Braintree service that day. After many years of DMU operation the latter line was electrified in 1977. Maldon goods shed survived until 1982 when it was carefully dismantled by members of the Stour Valley Railway Society.

BRAINTREE BRANCH

Class J19 0-6-0 No. 64646 from Cambridge cannot be said to have been specially groomed for this Railway Club brake van trip from Bishops Stortford to Braintree on 12th September 1959. The line lost its passenger traffic in 1952 and progressive closures to freight starting in 1966 saw final closure between Easton Lodge and Bishops Stortford six years later. The special train called at each station on the line and here at Dunmow participants are seen inspecting the signal box. At this time the somewhat steeply graded branch still saw the occasional excursion to Southend or Clacton, while at the beginning and end of terms, extra coaches were added to Cambridge Line service trains to work through to Felsted for the benefit of scholars at Felsted School. Felsted station was named Felstead until 1950. Part of the line near Braintree has now been adapted into a walkway.

The Bishops Stortford-Braintree branch opened in 1869 but this GER enamelled station sign at Rayne was probably a later 19th Century addition. Few such signs, once very popular, survived into BR days.

CAMBRIDGE-COLCHESTER LINE

For many years, except in wartime, the Cambridge University Railway Club had a tradition of running an 'Engine Driving and Firing Special' each spring between Linton and Haverhill on the Stour Valley line. The last surviving 'Intermediate' Class E4 2-4-0, No. 62785, stands in the lengthy bi-directional platform in Cambridge in readiness to set off on this excursion on 27th April 1958. At this time the through Sunday service between Cambridge and Colchester consisted only of one evening train each way via the Colne Valley line. The train consisted of a former GER main line coach of 1915 vintage and a Gresley LNER coach. A week later I photographed No. 62785 on the Mildenhall branch but by the following year it

was reduced to working the pick up goods train to and from Whittlesford. Withdrawn in December 1959 it was beautifully restored at Stratford the following year as GER No. 490 and forms part of the National Collection, being currently located at Bressingham Gardens, Norfolk.

Cambridge shed had cleaned up No. 62785 for this working and it is admired at Haverhill as the Locomotive Inspector supervises the real Fireman in getting forward some good lumps of coal. From recollection I know that the amateur firemen worked with great enthusiasm, though coal consumption erred on the high side and the pricker came into use during this station stop.

Peace reigns at Linton station as CURC members await the return of the special. Many GER rural stations were built in this yellow brick on a relatively grand scale and are now used as private dwellings. Notice a long forgotten feature of the country station,

the blue enamel sign reading 'YOU MAY TELEPHONE FROM HERE.'

Is this typical GER oil lamp cherished by some unknown enthusiast? The line from Marks Tey to Sudbury was opened by the Colchester, Stour Valley, Sudbury and Halstead Railway in 1849, but Linton was on the extension via Long Melford to Shelford, where it joined the Cambridge main line, opened by the GER in 1865.

A normal day's Stour Valley Line train, Class J15 0-6-0 No. 65446 heads a train of LNER stock on the 1.49 pm Colchester-Cambridge on 5th September 1959. It was recorded on the main line near Colchester and would diverge on to the branch at Marks Tey. Built in 1899, No. 65446 survived until the end of 1960. Currently the Stour Valley Railway Preservation Society, custodians of the preserved Class N7 0-6-2T No. 69621, are based at Chappel & Wakes Colne.
Photograph: K. L. Cook.

SAFFRON WALDEN BRANCH

Traditional push and pull engines on GE lines had been the little S.D. Holden Class F7 2-4-2Ts. Four of the twelve engines were withdrawn as early as 1931 but two remained at work on the Palace Gates-Seven Sisters shuttle service, which was taken over in 1938 by two Class G5 0-4-4Ts from the NER. In the same year the last James Holden Class G4 0-4-4T was withdrawn from service. The shuttle service ceased in 1942, the last F7 on GE lines then putting in two years service on the Epping-Ongar line. By 1944 a third Class G5 came south and the class was used on the Epping-Ongar service, moving in 1951 to Cambridge, where they were sub shedded at Saffron Walden, working the Audley End-Bartlow line, which connected with the Cambridge line at Audley End to serve Saffron Walden, running thence to Bartlow, where connection was made with the Stour Valley Line. Opened in 1865-6 by the independent Saffron Walden Railway, it was purchased by the GER in 1877. The line closed to passenger and freight traffic in 1964. The Bartlow platform was quite separate to those of the Stour Valley line and Class G5 0-4-4T No. 67322 was recorded there on 25th August 1956. The second coach is of interest, No. E63423E, built in 1897 for the Cromer express services and converted for push and pull operation in 1924 for the Palace Gates line, moving to Saffron Walden in 1951. Vacuum operated push and pull fitted Class N7 0-6-2Ts replaced the G5s in October 1956 but were in turn replaced by German built diesel railbuses two years later. These were used until the line closed. Examples of the railbuses survive on the North Norfolk and Keighley & Worth Valley Railways.

CAMBRIDGE

'Sandringham' Class B17/6 4-6-0 No. 61652 *Darlington* leaves Cambridge station with the Sunday 9.50 a.m. stopping train to Kings Cross. In the background can be seen Ivatt LMR Class 2MT 2-6-0 No. 46466 about to work an excursion to Clacton via the Colne Valley line. Five of these engines, built at Darlington in 1951, were allocated to GE lines, three at Cambridge and two at

Colchester. They augmented the surviving Class E4 2-4-0s and the passenger train fitted engines of Class J15, none of which were withdrawn as a result of the new arrivals. The Class E4 survivors were taken out of service between 1954 and 1959, while the last J15s were withdrawn in 1962, the last forty of the class built remaining intact until 1958.

Class D16/3 4-4-0 No. 62582 on Cambridge shed, 20th May 1957, having

worked the up 'Fenman' express from Kings Lynn to Ely. It returned to Ely with the 10.15 a.m. from Cambridge, no longer carrying the headboard. Note in the background the mechanical coaling plant erected in 1932.

Following the December 1956 electrification to Southend Victoria, a number of 4-6-0s were rendered surplus to immediate requirements and as a result Class B12/3s took the place of some of the D16/3 4-4-0s. Thus on 19th May 1957, Nos.

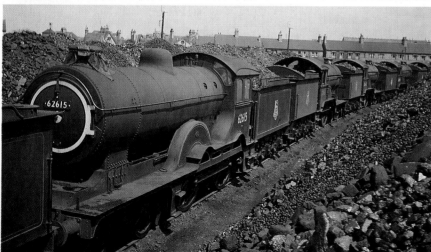

62513/21/34/39/45/76/88 and 62615 were in temporary store behind the coal stack at Cambridge shed. It is thought that most if not all these engines came out of store to work again, two being withdrawn later that year, the rest following in 1958. No. 62588 was the last survivor of twenty Class D16/3s fitted with piston valves. It will be noted from the most prominent engine, No. 62615, that not all the rebuilds lost their decorative valancing. These were the members of the class built as 'Super Clauds' with extended smokeboxes or rebuilt to that form. Only thirteen of these 4-4-0s were not rebuilt in some form, the last Class D15 survivor being No. 62509, withdrawn in 1952, in which year the last Class D16/2, No. 62590, was also condemned.

CAMBRIDGE

Class D16/3 4-4-0 No. 62529 in immaculate condition on Cambridge shed, 19th May 1957, having turned on shed after working the 9.50 a.m. from March via St. Ives. This engine as LNER No. 8878 was the most recent rebuild in May 1935 at the time of the celebration of the Silver Jubilee of King George V and with flags on the front it was among the principal exhibits at a Stratford Works Open Day to commemorate the event.

Class B17/6 4-6-0 No. 61600 *Sandringham,* which took its name from the Royal Estate on the GER Hunstanton branch, was the first of 48 engines of the class initially named after country houses situated near LNER lines. It is seen coming off Cambridge shed, 18th May 1957, passing Class D16/3 4-4-0 No. 62543 on shed. The first fifteen engines of the B17 Class were Westinghouse brake fitted, this being the GER standard equipment, and with much ex-GER stock still without vacuum gear at

the time of their construction. No. 61600 survived until July 1958. In this view it was about to work an up evening Liverpool Street train.

Hard working Class J15 0-6-0 No. 65477 earns its keep as Station Pilot at Cambridge, 24th June 1958, shunting the stock of an arrival from Kings Cross. Among the last of the class to be built, No. 65477 was withdrawn two years later. The steam leaks suggest that it was due for mechanical attention.

ENGINES OF GNR DESIGN

The large boilered Gresley Class K3 2-6-0s, introduced by the GNR in 1920, were not allowed on to GE lines south of March until 1938, after which they began to see widespread use, largely on heavy freight trains but to some extent on express passenger work first on the Cambridge main line and then on the Colchester route. Known to their crews as 'Jazzers', these modern engines — perpetuated by LNER construction between 1924 and 1937 — proved deservedly popular when new, less

so perhaps when they had built up a high mileage. Richard Hardy, then DMPS at Stratford, knowing my taste for footplate riding enquired whether I had ever had a ride on a K3. I had not done so and as they were then rostered on the 4.36 pm Liverpool Street-Bury St. Edmunds this was arranged and the late Len Theobald, Chief Locomotive Inspector, accompanied me. However, the Cambridge driver greeted me with the words 'You've come on the wrong night, Guv, we've got a ruddy old K3 to-night.' I then learnt that since the K3s were by then no longer in their prime, the Cambridge men had complained and the train had been re-diagrammed for a Class B1 4-6-0. I did not enlighten him as to

the reason for his having a K3 and in fact we had a very good run. 1924 built No. 61834 takes water at the north end of Cambridge station on this occasion, 16th June 1960.

Replaced on their home ground by the bigger Class K3 2-6-0s, some Class K2 2-6-0s were transferred to GE lines as early as 1924 and eventually there were twenty of them suitably fitted with Westinghouse brake. As with the K3s, they were equally at home on freight or passenger trains. However after the 1939-45 war, by which time most of them were based at Stratford on secondary freight duties, they were very run down. The design dated back to 1913 and when the new Thompson Class K1 2-6-0s rendered them superfluous on GE lines the GE men were not sorry to see them go. Thus No. 61771 was recorded on Boston shed, 24th June 1958. Withdrawal of the K2s took place between 1955 and 1961, while the last K3s survived until the end of 1962.

Another GNR class to see service on GE lines was the Class C12 4-4-2T, built 1898-1907. A small allocation came to Cambridge in 1938 to work the Audley End-Saffron Walden-Bartlow line, while three years earlier one had been used between Harwich and Parkeston Quay. In 1948-9 five of the class were fitted for push and pull working and these appeared on the Kings Lynn-South Lynn shuttle service, the Yarmouth South Town-Lowestoft and Beccles lines, while No. 67363 put in a brief appearance on the Epping-Ongar branch. When the Class G5 0-4-4Ts replaced the C12s on the Saffron Walden line in 1954 the non push and pull C12s displaced were used on such branches as Long Melford-Bury St. Edmunds and Thetford-Swaffham. Push and pull fitted No. 67366 was recorded at March shed, 19th May 1957, on its way from Doncaster Works to Yarmouth South Town about a year before withdrawal. The last survivors of the once fifty strong class were condemned in 1958. With a similar nickname to the bigger K3s, the K2s were known as 'Ragtimers'.

ELY

The cathedral city of Ely was reached in 1845 and two years later lines to Kings Lynn and Peterborough via March were opened followed by a line to Newmarket, making it a busy junction to the extent that a west curve was needed to permit running of freight trains between Norwich and Peterborough without reversal. Class D16/3 4-4-0 No. 62522 approaches Ely with the 2.03 p.m. from Kings Lynn via March, 26th April 1958. The GER favoured high signal posts in some locations and this Saxby & Farmer example contained the splitting distant signals for Ely North Junction. The arms refer to the lines to Norwich, Kings Lynn and March in order of importance. It survived until 1963 and was said to be listed for preservation, a fact not made known to the demolition gang.

Following a collision in fog at Stratford Western Junction between a Woolwich train and a goods engine in 1878, the decision was taken to introduce Fogging Indicators, the miniature arms of which repeated the aspects of the main signals and similarly had 'fail safe' counter balances. This set of fogging indicators reflects the signals for Ely North Junction above. Note at left the lever for placing detonators on the track. The arms are of GER design.

COLCHESTER

Edward Thompson succeeded Sir Nigel Gresley as Chief Mechanical Engineer of the LNER after Gresley's untimely death in 1941. Thompson set about implementing a standardisation policy which, because of wartime limitations, never proceeded as far as intended. One plan was to rebuild the 'Sandringhams' as two cylinder engines with an increased boiler pressure of 225 lbs. Only ten engines of the class were so treated and were known as Class B2, but most of the remaining 'Sandringhams' were fitted with the new boiler, standard with Thompson's Class B1 4-6-0, these being the B17/6 series. Class B2 4-6-0 No. 61632 *Belvoir Castle* was recorded in mellow autumn sun beside Colchester shed, 6th October 1956, at that time these engines were working on the slower services to London, experience with them on the Clacton express services having proved them to be very rough riding at speed. The class became extinct in 1959.

IPSWICH

By contrast with their LNER successors, the Class B12/3 4-6-0s have been described as 'riding like a carriage.' Their low axle loading and widespread route availability was advantageous while the late Cecil J. Allen recorded No. 8535 (later BR No. 61535) attaining 90 mph near Mellis on a 305 tons train load. When recorded at Ipswich shed on 22nd May 1957, No. 61572 was still to undergo a further major overhaul before withdrawal in 1961. It was privately purchased after withdrawal and as funds and skilled labour become available, is slowly being restored to working order at Weybourne on the North Norfolk Railway.

The Gresley designed Class J39 0-6-0s were introduced in 1926 and by 1941 there were 289 in service throughout the LNER system, coincidentally the same number as the older Class J15s, although built over a shorter period. Stratford had the largest number of the 74 engines allocated to the GE Section in 1939, twenty of which were fitted with Westinghouse brakes. These engines became familiar on passenger trains

notably in the summer service between London and Southend or Clacton, even appearing on longer main line duties, on which they managed to keep time even though experiencing some lively riding. Darlington built No. 64800 of 1929 was recorded on Ipswich shed on 22nd May 1957. It was being prepared to work a down freight to Felixstowe. The class became extinct in 1962 by which time none remained on the GE Section.

Ipswich shed had a good reputation for keeping engines clean and 1906-built Class J15 0-6-0 No. 65459 maintained this standard when it was rostered to work a Railway Club brake van special from Ipswich to Bentley, thence over the short branch to Hadleigh, opened in 1847. Remarkably, this once prosperous town enjoyed the facility of a slip coach working from Bentley, but all too briefly, in the winter service of 1876-7. It lost its passenger service in 1932, being closed altogether in 1965. No. 65459 was one of the series fitted with Westinghouse brake and vacuum ejector and also steam heating for passenger work. Recorded at Hadleigh on 9th June 1956, it survived until 1960.

KINGS LYNN

Class D16/3 4-4-0 No. 62582 leaves Kings Lynn for Ely on 23rd August 1958, giving an indication of the extensive layout that existed then. Behind the engine a Class J17 0-6-0 stands on the shed, while Stratford built 0-6-2T No. 69619, latterly with round topped firebox in the Class N7/4 series, stands at the limit of the shed yard. Note the tipped-over fogman's hut, showing a glimpse of the fogging indicators for the signal gantry.
(T. B. Owen)

The last survivor of the Class D16/3 4-4-0s, No. 62613, built at Stratford in 1923, later became a Class D16/2 engine and so retained the decorative valancing on rebuilding with round topped firebox. It is standing in Kings Lynn station on 1st June 1960 about to work to Hunstanton and back, the late Len Theobald beside the engine. At that time allocated to March, it survived until October 1960. On reaching Stratford Works for scrap it was not immediately broken up, later giving rise to false speculation that it was hidden somewhere in the works complex with a view to preservation; sadly this was untrue.

Class J17 0-6-0 No. 65560 about to work a freight train out of Kings Lynn on 1st June 1960. These engines numbered 90 and all except one were built with round topped fireboxes. Since the exception proved itself, all were eventually rebuilt with Belpaire fireboxes, the boilers being standard with those on the D15 'Claud Hamilton' 4-4-0s. As these were being reboilered this provided an adequate pool of spare boilers for the J17s. Superheaters were fitted from 1915 onwards. The class was introduced in the same year, 1900, as the pioneer 'Claud Hamilton' 4-4-0. All were eventually allocated throughout the GE and the last survivor, now preserved, was withdrawn in 1962.

FRAMLINGHAM BRANCH

The Framlingham branch, six miles in length, left the East Suffolk line at Wickham Market Junction and was opened in 1859. In common with many such lines, the station buildings were built on a grand scale; thus many long-closed stations in East Anglia survive in private ownership. The branch was engineered by Peto, Brassey & Betts with G.P. Bidder as the Engineer, both names being eminent in their fields in Victorian days. The line lost its passenger service in 1952 but through coaches, attached to or detached from main line trains at Ipswich, continued to serve the students of Framlingham College at the beginning and end of terms for another six years. I travelled on one such train on 2nd May 1958: three coaches attached to the rear of the 3.33 pm Liverpool Street-Yarmouth South Town, the train engine from Ipswich to Framlingham being Class B12/3 4-6-0 No. 61561. Printed tickets were still available. This picture

shows Class J15 0-6-0 No. 65389 preparing to work the branch freight back to Ipswich on 3rd May 1958. Note the water tank cast by the local engineering firm, Garrett's of Leiston and the typical goods shed.

The level crossing and its attendant keeper's house — no longer in use, the train crew now doing the work — are typical items of branch line scenery. Even the displaced crossing gate abandoned in the grass is familiar. Less so is the concrete World War II pill box in close proximity. Recorded on the Framlingham branch towards Parham on 3rd May 1958, the station house at Parham was on the market for what I considered to be then an astronomical figure. The branch lost its freight traffic in 1965.

No. 65389 shunts the coal siding adjacent to Marlesford station, itself typical of the splendour of these rural stations. The GER coach body, a Third Brake of 1877 vintage, used for storage on the station platform, is again a familiar sight. Note too the level crossing gates, longer but similar in design to those on the opposite page.

The Framlington branch freight was classed as a 'bonus trip', thus giving the

train crew the incentive to complete the job as quickly as possible. The fact that it was Cup Final day, 3rd May 1958, may also be the clue to the Fireman operating the point lever, a sight not normally seen even in a place as remote as Marlesford. On this Saturday morning the load was relatively

light, but a year earlier I recorded the same engine at Westerfield Junction with this train consisting of 33 wagons and a brake van. No. 65389 was built in 1890 and had two more years in service, its 70 year life span being a tribute to the soundness of the design.

SNAPE BRANCH

A small harbour on the River Alde existed before the Snape Maltings were built in the mid 1850s, at which time the 1½ mile branch was built by the East Suffolk Railway, opening in 1859. The branch left the main line at Snape Junction, three miles south of Saxmundham, north of the Framlingham branch with which it was worked. The line never had a scheduled passenger service.

The firm operating the Maltings went into voluntary liquidation in 1964 and the following year, work commenced to convert the largest and most modern malthouse into the concert hall to house the Aldeburgh Music Festival founded by the late Benjamin Britten. The concert hall and music school were opened by Her Majesty Queen Elizabeth in 1967. On 3rd May 1958 No. 65389 stands at the head of the sidings with some of the malthouses to be seen in the distance.

Having completed its work, No. 65389 crosses the timber trestle bridge over the River Alde to return to Ipswich, engine and brake van only. Class J15 was the largest engine permitted over this insubstantial bridge and even under the 13½ ton axle loading of No. 65389 there was some movement. The Goods Agent's house at Snape survives in private ownership.

WICKHAM MARKET

Following its work on the Framlingham branch, No. 65389 ran round the train at Wickham Market prior to completing its turn of duty on the Snape branch. The East Suffolk line between Ipswich and Lowestoft, after suffering several threats of closure, is still open and now worked by DMU Pay Trains in common with other surviving East Anglian branches. Its unique feature on GE lines is its simplified form of working with radio control.

GER CARRIAGES

Carriage No. E62445E was a standard 50ft Brake Third designed for use on the main lines. It was one of 102 such vehicles built between 1907 and 1917. Built at Stratford Works in 1915, it was recorded at Haverhill on 27th April 1958 and was withdrawn a few months later.

In a painted resemblance to the varnished teak livery, Carriage No. E62487E was built to a later design for main line work and had a 54ft body. It formed one of an order for 40 such coaches built by the Midland Railway Carriage & Wagon Company in 1920. Seen at Lowestoft on 22nd May 1957, it was withdrawn a year later.

LOWESTOFT

Long removed from its one time use as a suburban passenger engine, Class F6 2-4-2T No. 67229 was one of the final class of its type built by the GER, twenty engines entering service in 1911/12. It was recorded shunting at Coke Ovens Junction, Lowestoft on 22nd May 1957, at a time when the local fish traffic was still heavy. Express fish trains were worked by Lowestoft based Class K3 2-6-0s. No. 67229 was withdrawn the

following year, when the class became extinct.

Another important source of traffic at Lowestoft was the sleeper depot. The LNER had tried out a vertical boilered Sentinel engine in 1925, the design being based on the successful steam road locomotives. The railway was sufficiently impressed to order its first Sentinel the same year for this duty at Lowestoft. The design was considered economical and ideal for use on lightly laid track. Eventually the LNER had 56 engines of

the type in service throughout the system. No. 40 in the Departmental series, recorded at Lowestoft 22nd May 1957, was built in 1930 for the Traffic Department and only later transferred to departmental use. Two of the Departmental stock Sentinels of Class Y3, including No. 40, survived until 1964. No. 40 was built as LNER No. 63 in 1930. A similar engine of Class Y1/2, LNER No. 59 of 1933, was sold in 1961 to the Middleton Railway Preservation Society, Leeds, on which line it can still be seen in steam.

NORTH WOOLWICH OLD STATION MUSEUM

There were eight 'Coffee Pot' 0-4-0STs built for the GER over the years 1874-1903, becoming LNER Class Y5. Much of their work was carried out in London goods yards with tight curves on which duty they were replaced by A. J. Hill's Class Y4s. Others carried out dock or departmental duties at Ipswich, Lowestoft or Stratford. Only four survived into the LNER and one, No. 7230 (8081 under Thompson's 1946 renumbering), was immaculately kept at Stratford and attended many rolling stock exhibitions on the LNER system. It was withdrawn in 1948, but one still survived, GER No. 229 sold to the Admiralty in 1917 for use at Chepstow and later bought by the Fairfield Shipbuilding & Engineering Co., based nearby. The Company intended to preserve it but it was stored in the open becoming increasingly rusty. Finally a home for it was found at the Great Eastern Railway Museum established by the Passmore Edwards Trust at the old North Woolwich Station. There it has been immaculately restored displaying the eye catching Royal Blue livery of the GER. At this point it should be noted that those interested in GER matters are well catered for by the GER Society, very active in dissemination of information on the line. Enquiries may be directed care of the North Woolwich Old Station Museum.